Beat Estate Tax Forever

Beat Estate Tax Forever

The Unprecedented $5 Million Opportunity in 2012

*Protect the Family Business,
the Farm,
your Lifetime's Work*

Michael Gilfix

Library of Congress Control Number: 2012905732
ISBN: Hardcover   978-1-4691-8733-4
               Softcover   978-1-4691-8732-7
               Ebook   978-1-4691-8734-1

This book was printed in the United States of America.

To order additional copies of this book, contact:
Xlibris Corporation
1-888-795-4274
www.Xlibris.com
Orders@Xlibris.com
111820

Contents

Dedication

I dedicate this book to Myra Gerson Gilfix, whose advice, support, and insights are a constant source of clarity and inspiration.

Acknowledgments

Particularly when a book is time sensitive, help from others is essential. Fortunately, I had the help I needed. Mark Gerson Gilfix found the publisher and negotiated terms of publication.

I received excellent and timely substantive suggestions from tax attorney Francis A. La Poll, Myra Gerson Gilfix, and Ellen Cookman. They also provided assistance with editing, as did Jamie Arielle Gerson Gilfix. Jamie also served as Production Manager, kept us on schedule, and took care of countless communications with our publisher.

My friend and Stanford Law School classmate Jeffrey Yablon annually publishes a wonderful book, <u>As Certain as Death: Quotations about Taxes</u>. I liberally borrowed quotes contained in his book. I also borrowed many words of Len Tillem, a remarkably insightful radio show host in California's Northern Bay Area.

Insurance professional Jack Bellevue helped me with insurance illustrations. Don Maruska, my good friend and business coach, offered practical and important guidance about the best approach to maximize success at every level. Many of my friends and colleagues, too many to name here, helped craft an effective title for this book and added extremely useful advice about its circulation and impact. Sincere thanks to all of them.

I thank and acknowledge you, the reader, for sharing this book with others and ensuring its broad distribution.

Finally, I thank our excellent staff at Gilfix & La Poll Associates for their ongoing patience and commitment to quality services for our client community.

Disclaimer

This book is presented solely for educational purposes. The author is not offering it as legal or other professional services advice. Every individual is different and the advice and strategies contained herein may not be suitable for your situation. You should seek the services of a competent professional before implementing a plan to address estate or other tax exposure. Examples are fictional. Any likeness to actual persons, either living or dead, is strictly coincidental.

Glossary of Legal Terms in this Book

AB Trust—A type of Revocable Living Trust used by married couples. In this type of living trust, two trusts (trust A and trust B) are created at the time the first spouse dies. By dividing the couple's estate into two trusts at the first death, each spouse can pass the maximum amount of property allowed to avoid federal estate taxes. One trust, usually trust A, is often referred to as the Survivor's Trust or Marital Deduction Trust, and the other trust, usually trust B, is often referred to as the Exemption Trust, Bypass Trust, or Credit Shelter Trust.

Advance Health Care Directive—A document established by an individual (the principal) granting another person (the agent) the right and authority to handle matters related to the health care of the principal.

Annual Exclusion—The amount of property the IRS allows a person to give to another person during a calendar year before a gift tax is assessed and/or a gift tax return must be filed. The amount is increased periodically. There is no limit to the number of people you can give gifts to which qualify for the annual exclusion. To qualify for the annual exclusion, the gift must be one that a recipient can enjoy immediately and have full control over.

Annuity—The periodic payment of a definite sum of money, with such payments to continue for life or for a definite number of years.

Asset Protection—Protecting your property from legal problems and taxes during your life and after your death.

Assets—All types of property which can be made available for the payment of debts.

Basis—A tax term, which refers to the original or acquisition value of a property, used to determine the amount of tax that will be assessed. The basis is deducted from the sales price of the property when it is sold to determine the profit or loss.

Beneficiary—The person(s) or organization(s) who receive(s) the benefits of trust property held under the terms of a trust.

Bequest—An old legal term meaning a gift or property given under the terms of a will.

Bypass Trust—see Exemption Trust

Charitable Lead Trust (CLT)—An irrevocable trust where a charity receives a certain amount of income during a fixed term. When the term expires, the remainder is distributed to individual beneficiaries.

Charitable Remainder Trust (CRT)—An irrevocable trust where individual beneficiaries receive a certain amount of income during a fixed term. When the fixed term expires, the remainder is donated to a charity.

Charitable Remainder Unitrust (CRUT)—A Charitable Remainder Trust where individual beneficiaries receive a fixed percentage (e.g. 4%) of the trust principal each year during the term of the trust.

Charitable Remainder Annuity Trust (CRAT)—A Charitable Remainder Trust where individual beneficiaries receive a fixed dollar amount (e.g. $40,000) each year during the term of the trust.

Charitable Trust—An irrevocable trust having a charitable organization as a lifetime beneficiary (Charitable Lead Trust) or a death beneficiary (Charitable Remainder Trust).

CLT—See Charitable Lead Trust

Community Property—Some state laws require that all assets acquired during a marriage belong equally to both spouses, except for gifts and inheritances given specifically to one spouse. The eight states with such laws, including California, are known as community property states.

Consideration—Something which has value, such as real or personal property or a promise given in exchange for another promise.

CRAT—See Charitable Remainder Annuity Trust

Credit Shelter Trust—See Exemption Trust

CRT—See Charitable Remainder Trust

Crummey Trust—An irrevocable trust that allows a limited withdrawal by the trust's beneficiary during a short time period each year. Such trusts qualify for the annual gift tax exclusion. The beneficiary typically does not withdraw the gift during the withdrawal period, and the money remains in the trust until the beneficiary reaches the designated distribution age. Crummey trusts are often used in conjunction with life insurance and Irrevocable Life Insurance Trusts (ILITs).

CRUT—See Charitable Remainder Unitrust

Decedent—The person who has died.

Death taxes—Taxes levied on the property of a deceased person. Federal death taxes are usually referred to as estate taxes. Local and state death taxes are often referred to as inheritance taxes, or simply death taxes.

Deed—A written document used to evidence ownership and/or transfer title to real estate.

Disclaimer—The refusal of a beneficiary to accept property willed to him. When a disclaimer is made, the property is generally transferred to the person next in line under the will. A disclaimer is also called a renunciation.

Donor—A person who makes a gift.

Durable Power of Attorney—A document established by an individual (the principal) granting another person (the agent) the right and authority to handle the financial and other affairs of the principal. The Durable Power of Attorney survives through the period of incompetency of the principal.

Dynasty Trust—A trust designed to pass down family wealth for many generations while avoiding transfer taxes (estate tax and generation-skipping tax) to the greatest extent possible.

Estate—The aggregate of all assets and debts held (owned) by an individual during his or her life or at the time of his or her death.

Estate Planning—The process by which a person plans for transferring his or her assets at death.

Estate Taxes—Taxes imposed on the "privilege" of transferring property by reason of death. Estate tax is most commonly used in reference to the tax imposed by the Federal Government rather than the state government. Estate taxes are intended to raise revenue for the government and break up a family's wealth, so that the nation's wealth doesn't concentrate in the hands of a few families.

Exemption Trust—An irrevocable trust that captures the maximum level of estate tax protection for the first spouse to die, holding the assets of that spouse from a married couple's estate. See AB Trust for further explanation.

Family Foundation—An entity into which assets are transferred, removing those assets from your taxable estate. Family members can serve as officers and directors of the foundation, and help to achieve its charitable objectives.

Family Limited Partnership (FLP)—A way to transfer business assets to the next generation at a discounted rate, while retaining control over the assets and/or a right to income.

Family Protection Trust (FPT)—See Dynasty Trust

FLP—See Family Limited Partnership

FPT—See Family Protection Trust

Generation Skipping Transfer (GST) Tax—A federal tax imposed on large amounts of money given or left to a grandchild or great-grandchild. Its purpose is to keep families from avoiding the estate tax that would be due if the oldest generation left property to their children, who then left it to their children (the original giver's grandchildren).

Generation Skipping Transfer (GST) Trust—See Dynasty Trust

Gift Taxes—Taxes levied by the Federal Government on gifts. Gift taxes and estate taxes have been "merged" into a single tax called the "unified tax."

Grantor—See Settlor

Grantor Retained Annuity Trust (GRAT)—An irrevocable trust where the grantor of the trust property (e.g., highly-appreciating stock) receives a fixed income stream during a term of years, and the remaining assets are distributed tax-free or at a discount to the beneficiaries.

Grantor Retained Interest Trust (GRIT)—An irrevocable trust where the grantor of the trust property (e.g., a personal residence) receives an income for a fixed period of time.

Gross Estate—The total value of an estate at the date of the decedent's death. The value is determined before debts and other "deductions" are subtracted from the estate value.

Heir—A person entitled to inherit a portion of the estate of a person who has died without a Will.

IDIT—See Intentionally Defective Irrevocable Trust

ILIT—See Irrevocable Life Insurance Trust

Inheritance Tax—A tax imposed upon the transfer of property from a deceased person's estate. "Inheritance Tax" is a term which is usually applied to the taxes charged by a state, whereas the taxes imposed by the Federal Government are usually referred to as estate taxes.

Intentionally Defective Irrevocable Trust (IDIT)—An irrevocable trust in which the grantor retains a controlling interest in trust-owned assets. It often offers significant tax advantages.

Inter Vivos Revocable Trust—One name for a living trust. "Inter vivos" is Latin for "between the living."

Irrevocable Life Insurance Trust (ILIT)—A type of irrevocable trust used to hold life insurance. When a life insurance policy is held in an insurance trust, it is protected from estate taxes when the insured dies, provided the trust is established properly, managed properly, and the insured does not retain any "incidents of ownership."

Irrevocable Trust—A trust that cannot be changed, canceled, or "revoked" once it is set up. A "living trust" is not an irrevocable trust. Insurance trusts, GRITs and Dynasty Trusts are examples of irrevocable trusts. Irrevocable trusts are treated by the IRS very differently than revocable trusts.

Insurance Trust—An irrevocable trust used to hold insurance and pass it on to heirs without any estate taxes on the death benefits of the policy.

Issue—A legal term used in wills and trusts meaning one's children, grandchildren, etc., either through birth or adoption.

Life Estate—The right to have all of the benefit from a property during one's lifetime. The person with the right does not own the property, and when he or she dies, the property is not included in his or her estate.

Limited Liability Company (LLC)—A type of business whose owners actively participate in the organization's management and are protected against personal liability for the organization's debts and obligations.

Limited Liability Partnership (LLP)—A type of partnership in which individual partners are protected against personal liability for certain partnership liabilities.

Living Trust—A type of revocable trust used in estate planning to avoid probate, help in situations of incompetency, and allow "smooth" management of assets after the death of the grantor or person who established the trust. The trust can be effective in eliminating or reducing estate taxes for married couples. Revocable living trusts are established during the life of the grantor, who retains the right to the income and principal and the right to amend or revoke the trust. When the grantor dies, the trust becomes irrevocable and acts as a substitute for a traditional will.

LLC—See Limited Liability Company

LLP—See Limited Liability Partnership

Marital Deduction—The unlimited deduction allowed under federal estate tax law for all qualifying property passing from the estate of the deceased spouse to the surviving spouse. The value of the property passing to the surviving spouse under the marital deduction is "deducted" from the deceased spouse's estate before federal estate taxes are calculated on the estate. Proper planning and use of the deduction allows more property to pass estate tax-free to the family.

Marital Deduction Trust—See Survivor's Trust

Personal Property—Property other than real estate (land and permanent structures on the land). Cars, furniture, securities, bank accounts, and animals are examples of personal property.

Personal Residence Trust (PRT)—See Grantor Retained Interest Trust

Pour-over Will—A will which contains a clause that transfers some or all of the assets that pass through the will into a trust for final distribution from the trust. The will's assets are said to "pour over" into the trust.

Power of Appointment—The power given to a person, by appointment in a will or a trust, to distribute the property that passes through the will or trust at the discretion of the person appointed. Other than to give the appointed person the authority to make the distribution, the will or trust doesn't make distribution of the property.

Prenuptial Agreement—A contract between two potential marriage partners specifying how the property owned by each prior to marriage and owned individually or jointly during marriage will be divided should the couple divorce.

Probate—The legal process which facilitates the transfer of a deceased person's property whether they leave a will or die without a will.

PRT—See Personal Residence Trust

QDOT—See Qualified Domestic Trust

QPRT—See Qualified Personal Residence Trust

Qualified Domestic Trust (QDOT)—A type of trust that allows taxpayers who are not U.S. citizens to claim the marital deduction for estate tax purposes.

Qualified Personal Residence Trust (QPRT)—See Grantor Retained Interest Trust

Reversionary Interest—An interest that a grantor transferred to another person or entity, but which will revert back to the grantor if and when a certain event occurs.

Revocable Trust—A trust which can be amended or revoked by the person(s) who established the trust.

Revocable Living Trust—See Living Trust

Real Property—Land and attachments to the land, such as buildings, fences, etc.

Rule Against Perpetuities (RAP)—An old legal rule that if a person is designated as the future transferee, or beneficiary, of a property, that property must be transferred to him or her not later than 21 years after the death of the transferor.

Settlor—A person who establishes a trust. The term settlor is used interchangeably with the terms "trustor" and "grantor."

Stepped-up Basis—The new basis established for a property after the owner's death if the property is in the owner's estate.

Successor Trustee—The trustee who takes over when the initial trustee can no longer function.

Surviving Spouse—The husband or wife that lives after the death of his or her spouse.

Survivor's Trust—A revocable trust that contains the surviving spouse's property interest, over which that spouse has total control. See AB Trust for further explanation.

Taxable Estate—The portion of an estate that is subject to federal or state estate taxes.

Trust—A legal document in which property is held and managed by a trustee for the benefit of another known as a beneficiary. A trust is a relationship in which property is held by one person for the benefit of another.

Trust Corpus or Res—The property of a trust.

Trustee—The person or institution that manages the trust property under the terms of the trust.

Trustor—See Settlor

Unified Credit—A tax credit is given to each person by the IRS to be used during his or her life or after his or her death. The tax credit equals the amount of tax (gift or estate) which is assessed on the exemption equivalent value of property. It is considered the "unified" credit because it applies to both gift taxes and estate taxes and results from the IRS's effort to unify these two taxes or make them consistent.

Valuation Discount—A discount or reduction in the value of an asset for estate valuation purposes. It can be based on a lack of marketability, limited control, loss of control, or the inability to quickly sell the asset at a known price with minimal transaction costs.

Preface: Why This Book is Vitally Important for You and Your Family

Most of us don't like to think about the two great inevitabilities: *death and taxes*. Yet, that is what this book is about: the planning you can do to protect virtually all of your assets from the punishing estate tax.

This is a book that needed to be written because, in 2012 only, we have the most remarkable tax avoidance opportunity in American history—and hardly anyone is talking about it. The *Wall Street Journal* called it "The $5 Million Tax Break." My goal is to make you aware of what you can do to protect your estate for the benefit of your children and grandchildren. Doing so can save millions of dollars—the estate you built up over a lifetime—for their benefit.

If you do nothing, 30% or 40% of your estate could go to the U.S. Treasury as "estate taxes" upon your passing. You will roll over in your grave! And you will only have yourself to blame. You have the opportunity to avoid this tax. To take advantage of the opportunity, you have to act now.

I worked very hard to make this book understandable. The use of some "legalese," however, is inevitable. This is why I include a Glossary that defines many of the terms that are used in this book. Refer to it often.

Also for the sake of simplicity and understanding, I recurrently refer to the "$5 million" exemption or planning opportunity. This figure is used in the text and any examples because it is a simple, round figure. It makes the examples easier to understand. In fact, the level of gift and estate tax protection is actually **$5,120,000** in 2012. The level of estate and gift tax protection was set at $5 million in 2011 and, pursuant to terms of the legislation, increased to $5,120,000 in 2012 because it is indexed for inflation.

This means that you can actually give away a minimum of $5,120,000 this year. That's another $120,000 that you can protect for your family if you are so fortunate as to have a large estate.

This book is for you if your "estate" is over $1 million. You don't have to have a $5 million estate to benefit. Starting next year, in 2013, everything over $1 million is exposed to the voracious estate tax. So if your estate is $1.5 million or $2 million, you must either plan to avoid that tax or your estate will suffer.

Finally, and although I explain most of the planning options that are available to you, I made no effort to identify every option and every variation. Time, space, and good judgment place limits on how many details can realistically be absorbed.

Tax and estate planning, needless to say, is a complicated process. While a good fiction writer abhors giving away a story's conclusion in an introduction, I revel in giving it away: **You need to act, to work with an experienced estate and tax attorney to help you win the tax planning challenge.**

Contact our office, Gilfix and La Poll Associates, of Palo Alto, California, at www.gilfix.com for professional assistance or more information.

Chapter 1: 2012
An Unprecedented Year of Opportunity

*"The $5 Million Tax Break"—Wall Street Journal,
January 29, 2011*

The estate tax is a rapacious tax. It taxes assets on which you have already been taxed. While you earned it, you paid income tax. When you sold it, you paid capital gains tax. At the time of your death, the estate tax steps in and takes thousands, hundreds of thousands, or even millions of dollars.

This year, 2012, presents a remarkable opportunity from a tax planning perspective. You can transfer $5 million[1] or more to the next generation–$10 million or more if you are a couple–without paying any tax.[2] If death occurs this year, you can leave up to $5 million to your children, grandchildren, or others without any estate tax whatsoever.

More importantly, for the first time in American tax history, you can alternatively give away a minimum of $5 million without paying any gift tax! It is particularly powerful because of low asset values, low interest rates, and "valuation discounts" that are currently available.

---

[1]   Remember: The actual amount in 2012 is $5,120,000. We nevertheless and consistently refer to $5 million for the sake of simplicity.

[2]   This became the law when the Tax Relief, Unemployment Insurance Reauthorization, and Job Creation Act of 2010 was passed by Congress and signed by the President on December 17, 2010.

This opportunity disappears in 2013, when the level of gift and estate tax protection plummets to only $1 million. To make it even worse, the effective level of estate tax increases from the current 35% to as high as 60%. These enormous changes are shown in Chart A.

CHART A:
Estate and Gift Tax Protection
2012 and 2013 Comparison[3]

2012	2013
Estate Tax Exemption: $5,000,000	Estate Tax Exemption: $1,000,000
Gift Tax Exemption: $5,000,000	Gift Tax Exemption: $1,000,000
Estate Tax and Gift Tax Rate: up to 35%	Estate Tax and Gift Tax Rate: up to 60%

Example 1-1: Single and $2 million

A single person with a $2 million estate (a house, a modest IRA, and $400,000 in savings) dies in 2013. Only $1 million is protected from estate tax. The estate tax exceeds $345,000.

---

[3]   This chart illustrates what will happen in 2013 unless there is new tax legislation. If there is new legislation in 2012, the exemption amount could be $2 million, $3.5 million, or some other amount.

<u>Example 1-2: Couple and $5 million</u>

A couple with a $5 million estate dies in 2013. Only $2 million is protected from estate tax. The estate tax is $1,275,800.

* * *

Giving away your assets is never easy. It runs counter to many of our instincts. But if doing so could save your family a fortune, should it not be considered?

"I worked all my life to build what I have.
I'll be damned if I'll let it all go out the window
on my death."
—B.T., a client of the Gilfix & La Poll office

Chapter 2: What Is In Your "Estate?"

A. What Is Included

Surprise! It includes everything you own, and perhaps more.

Let's be clear about what is in your estate. It may be more than you think.

Most obviously, assets titled in your name, or in your revocable trust, are yours and are included in your taxable estate.

Perhaps less obviously, the following are also included:

- IRAs, 401(k)s, and other retirement accounts.

- The "death benefit" value of life insurance if you own it, pay premiums, or have any control over it.

- Accounts you funded and over which you serve as "custodian." These might be accounts you set up for your children or grandchildren and into which you have made $13,000 "annual exclusion" gifts.

- Assets in your name or in your revocable trust.

- Trust assets that are not yours, but where you have a "general power of appointment." You have this power if you can decide where the assets pass on your death. You may be given this power by others and be unaware of it.

- Assets you are likely to inherit from a parent or others. Include life insurance policies and IRA and other retirement accounts where you are the designated beneficiary.

- Life insurance policies you give to others during the three years immediately preceding your death.

- Property in which a "life estate" is held.

- Property which was transferred, but the transferor retains the power to revoke the transfer or retains a "power of appointment" or "reversionary interest."

- Some annuities.

- Some property held in joint tenancy.

This list is not comprehensive. Other assets can sneak into your estate because of arcane tax laws that are designed to–guess what–increase your tax liability.

As noted above, life insurance benefits may be included in your taxable estate, even though you did not own the policy. Life insurance proceeds are generally included in your estate if the benefits are payable to your estate, if you were the owner of the life insurance policy, or if you had any "incidents of ownership" over the life insurance policy (such as the power to change the beneficiary designation). Similarly, bank accounts or other financial instruments that are in your name and titled "payable on death" (POD) or that "transfer on death" (TOD) are usually included in the taxable estate.

* * *

B. Estimating Your Estate

Here is a worksheet that will let you figure out the size of your taxable estate.

Hint: do not "lowball" the value of your home and other real property. At the time of your passing, an objective appraisal determines the value of real property. Be realistic and, if anything, optimistic about the values.

CHART B:
Valuing Your Estate

Residence (less mortgage) .... $_____

Total additional Real Property,
    less mortgages..................................... $_____

Total Stock, Bonds, Cash, etc .... $_____

Total IRAs & Retirement plans .... $_____

Total Life Insurance (face amounts)............. $_____

LLC, S or C corporations,
    LLP, FLP interests .... $_____

Total Business Interests (less debts)............ $_____

Expected Inheritances .... $_____

TOTAL ESTIMATED ESTATE $_____

Surprised at how large your estate is? The fact is that most of us have estates larger than we would have guessed or estimated.

If you are single, does the Total Estimated Estate exceed $1 million? If you are a couple, does the Total Estimated Estate exceed $2 million? If the answer is "Yes," read on. This book can save you and your family a fortune.

Chapter 3: The Estate Tax and Gift Tax—How Do They Fit Together?

A. Estate Tax

The estate tax came into being nearly 100 years ago, and the gift tax followed shortly thereafter. The exemption amount started at $50,000 in 1916, remained relatively steady until 1977 when it jumped to $120,000, and has been increasing ever since. The maximum estate tax rate started at 10%, but by 1935 it had increased to 70%, hitting 77% for the years 1941 to 1976. The rate started declining in 1982, and is currently at 35%. Despite its variation, and notwithstanding its elimination for one year (2010), the estate tax is a permanent fixture in our approach to taxation and intergenerational transfers of assets.

A selective history of the estate tax—since 1990—illustrates the relative volatility of this tax. Its relative unpredictability underscores both the difficulty of planning and the need for planning. As "Chart C" shows, the amount protected from estate tax has varied from year to year and with the winds of political change. The tax rate has also changed from time to time.

B. Gift Tax

Also included in Chart C is the "Gift Tax Exemption" that has been available during these same years. This is the amount of money which, in addition to the "annual exclusion," can be given away without paying any gift or transfer tax. Note that the maximum gift tax exemption amount was $1 million per person from 2002 until 2010, even while the estate tax exemption was dramatically increasing and even eliminated for deaths occurring in 2010. But for a brief two-year period, ending on December 31, 2010, the President and Congress removed the lower $1 million cap on tax-free gifts, replacing it with the $5 million per person gift limit.

On January 1, 2013, both the gift and estate tax protections plummet to only $1 million. This low figure will only be avoided if Congress enacts new tax legislation. How likely is that in this political climate and in 2012, an election year?

CHART C:
Estate and Gift Tax Protection 1990-2013

Calendar Year	Highest Estate Tax Rate	Estate Tax Exemption	Highest Gift Tax Rate	Gift Tax Exemption
1990-1997	55%	$600,000	55%	$600,000
1998	55%	$625,000	55%	$625,000
1999	55%	$650,000	55%	$650,000
2000	55%	$675,000	55%	$675,000
2001	55%	$675,000	55%	$675,000
2002	50%	$1,000,000	50%	$1,000,000
2003	49%	$1,000,000	49%	$1,000,000
2004	48%	$1,500,000	48%	$1,000,000
2005	47%	$1,500,000	47%	$1,000,000
2006	46%	$2,000,000	46%	$1,000,000
2007	45%	$2,000,000	45%	$1,000,000
2008	45%	$2,000,000	45%	$1,000,000
2009	45%	$3,500,000	45%	$1,000,000
2010	35%	Unlimited	35%	$1,000,000
2011	35%	$5,000,000	35%	$5,000,000
2012	**35%**	**$5,000,000***	**35%**	**$5,000,000***
2013	**55%**	**$1,000,000**	**55%**	**$1,000,000**

* Reminder: We use $5,000,000 for simplicity. The actual estate and gift tax protection in 2012 is $5,120,000.

*"For the first time in American tax history,
an individual can give away at least $5,000,000
without paying gift or any other tax."*
—M.G.

It cannot be said too often: this $5 million tax-free giving opportunity disappears at midnight December 31, 2012. It is possible that Congress and the White House will agree on new legislation to avoid this precipitous erosion of opportunity. The President proposed $3.5 million in his 2013 budget. Congressional leaders are all over the map. It is difficult to be optimistic about this.

From a planning perspective, remember that each individual can give away $5 million or pass along $5 million upon death, depending on the year. This means that a couple can pass along a minimum of $10 million in 2012. With sophisticated planning, as discussed in Chapter 8, dramatically more can be removed from your taxable estate.

C. The Annual Exclusion

No discussion of gifting is complete without attention to the annual exclusion. Best known as the (outdated) $10,000 gifting opportunity, it is now $13,000. It lets each of us give away up to $13,000 per year to as many people as we like, without having to report it to the IRS. For further discussion, see Chapter 6, section A.

"A gift (beyond $13,000) exhausts estate tax protection, dollar for dollar."
—M.G.

If a gift is made in excess of the annual exclusion to any one person, it must be reported to the IRS on a Gift Tax Return, Form 709. The IRS effectively keeps track of such gifts because the gift and estate tax protections are "unified." This means that you have a choice: you can either give away $5 million in 2012 and pay no gift tax or you can die in 2012 and your estate pays no estate tax on the first $5 million in your estate. You cannot do both. If you give away $5 million this year, you will have zero estate tax protection remaining. Every penny in your estate at the time of death will be exposed to estate tax, which will be as high as 55%, or even 60%, commencing in 2013.

"Bad Plan: Die in 2012.
Good Plan: Gift in 2012."
—M.G.

Chapter 4: The Important, but Limited, Role of Revocable Trusts in Estate Tax Planning

Myth: A trust avoids estate tax

Revocable living trusts, also known as *inter vivos* trusts, are excellent planning tools. They ensure the avoidance of probate, which can be unnecessarily costly, time-consuming, and public. They ensure ongoing management of your estate by trusted individuals if you become incapacitated or upon your passing. They do not, however, ensure the avoidance of estate tax.

Single person: for a single person, a revocable trust achieves *no estate tax planning whatsoever*. With or without a trust, an individual can pass along $5 million without estate tax exposure if the death occurs in 2012. In 2013, $1 million is protected, again with or without a revocable trust.

Married couple: for a married couple, a properly drafted revocable trust can protect the combined maximum level of protection for each spouse. This is $10 million if deaths occur in 2012. It will be only $2 million if deaths occur in 2013 or later. To achieve this protection, alternative approaches can be taken. The most typical approach is to use an AB trust, which mandates the division of the estate into two sub-trusts after the first death. It captures the maximum level of estate tax protection for each spouse, effectively doubling the amount that can pass tax-free.

The AB trust avoids estate tax after the first death because of the "marital deduction." This means that a married person can leave any amount of money to or for the benefit of the surviving spouse without exposure to any estate tax whatsoever.

This same result—avoiding all estate tax at the first spouse's death while capturing the basic level of estate tax protection—can be achieved in other ways. Particularly on the East Coast, in non-community property states like New York, estate planning attorneys more typically prepare separate trusts, one for each spouse. The same tax avoidance result is achieved; the same exposure remains.

Example 4-1: Bill Yates and the Marital Deduction

Bill Yates dies and leaves $3 billion to the surviving spouse, Belinda. Because of the "marital deduction," there is no estate tax at the time of his death. The marital deduction provides that any amount of money can be left to a surviving spouse without exposure to estate tax. Unless proactive planning steps are taken, the IRS will collect estate taxes when Belinda dies.

The following illustration (Illustration I) shows what happens with a $10 million estate if the first death occurs in 2012 and the married couple has an AB Trust. Note that there are no estate taxes whatsoever.

ILLUSTRATION I
AB Trust—Estate Tax Protection in 2012

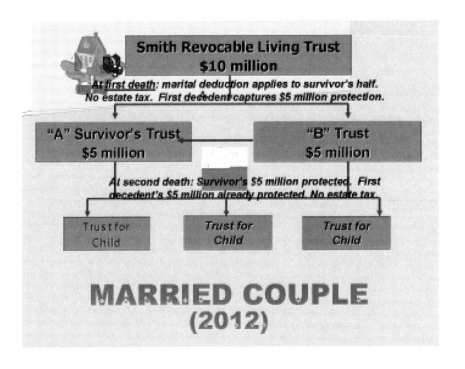

Illustration II shows what happens with a $10 million estate if the first death occurs in 2013. Note that only $2 million is protected from estate tax. The tax can exceed $4 million.

ILLUSTRATION II
AB Trust—Estate Tax Protection in 2013

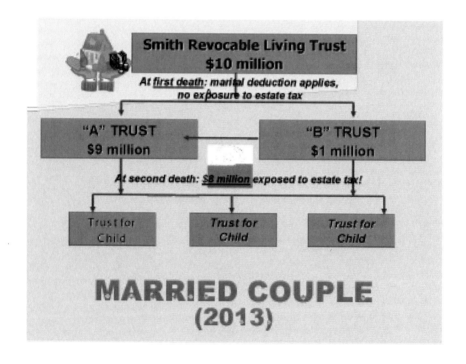

What if your estate is less than $10 million? See Illustration III, which shows the tax exposure in 2013 if you have an AB Trust and, for example, a $4 million estate. As you can see, $2 million is exposed to estate tax!

ILLUSTRATION III
AB Trust—Estate Tax Protection in 2013

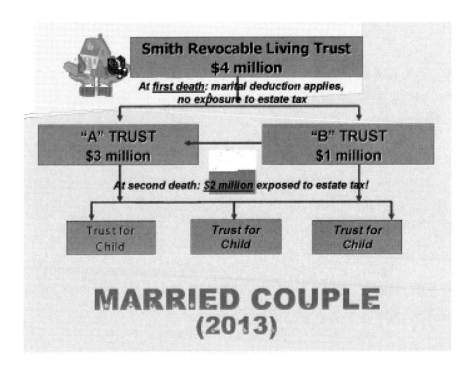

The 2013 (and beyond) result is over $1 million in estate tax to be paid. I cannot over-emphasize: you do not have to have a $5 million or $10 million estate. If your estate exceeds $2 million, you will have exposure in and after 2013. This tax exposure is avoidable by taking protective action in 2012, as described in Chapters 6-9.

*   *   *

Noncitizen surviving spouse: noncitizens may not take advantage of the marital deduction. However, in 2012, there is an annual gifting exclusion of $139,000 for gifts made to a non-U.S. citizen spouse. Furthermore, a noncitizen may take full advantage of the $5 million gifting opportunity in 2012. To address estate tax exposure, when the surviving spouse is not a citizen, a qualified domestic trust (QDOT) is typically appropriate.

Same-sex couples: Because this marital deduction principle is in federal estate tax law, same-sex partners cannot take advantage of the marital deduction. Other planning steps must be taken to minimize estate tax exposure.

Chapter 5: You Can Plan to Avoid the Estate Tax. Overcoming Inertia; Overcoming Objections.

"You can protect the family home. You can protect the family business. You can probably protect everything."
—M.G.

A. Addressing Objections

Most people do nothing to avoid the estate tax. This delights the IRS and the U.S. Treasury, which receives your estate tax money. It does not delight your children. It would make you roll over in your grave if you could see it happen. If you think about it, not planning is a way of planning to make substantial gifts to the IRS.

Here are the most typical reasons, beyond the powers of inertia and ignorance, why people fail to plan.

1. You may say "I'll be gone. What do I care?"
2. You may be unwilling to pay legal fees.
3. You may be unwilling to give up control of your assets.
4. You may feel that you need to keep your money for travel, enjoyment, and the cost of long-term care.

Let's address these very logical thoughts.

1. What do I care? Let the kids deal with it.

"Death is the most convenient time to tax rich people."
—David Lloyd George

It is your privilege to do as little or as much planning as you wish. You must, however, consider the consequences of inaction. The following examples may surprise you. I admit it: They are designed to shake you out of complacency.

Example 5-1: the $1 million house

Mrs. Jones has lived simply all her life. Thirty years ago, she bought a nice house in a wonderful neighborhood. She reluctantly acknowledges that it is worth $1 million in today's market. She also built up a $400,000 IRA. She has another $200,000 in savings and investments. She lives frugally and does not see herself as a "rich person." She had a local attorney prepare a living trust, which appropriately holds title to all of her assets except the IRA. Mrs. Jones dies in

2013. She would be shocked to know that her two children *will lose some $300,000 because of the estate tax.* This tax will likely force her children to sell the home, which Mrs. Jones told them to keep in the family.

Example 5-2: the $1 million life insurance policy

Mr. and Mrs. Smith feel that they have a modest estate. They own their home and a small cabin in the mountains. They have two savings accounts and a stock portfolio valued at $250,000. These assets are valued at $1.5 million. They created an AB trust and believe that there will be no estate tax.

They have a $1 million life insurance policy naming their children as beneficiaries. They never thought of this as an asset because "it goes to the children." They were also told that the life insurance policy is "tax-free" when they purchased it and made their premium payments. The information they were given about tax was only half right. Receipt of a life insurance death benefit is free from income tax exposure. Unfortunately, however, the $1 million death benefit is counted as part of their taxable estate.

Because their estate is therefore valued at $2.5 million, the *estate tax will be approximately $250,000* at the time of the second death.

"You may not care, but your kids will.
They may even be willing to pay for good advice!
After all, the planning is for them."
—M.G.

Example 5-3: the $5 million estate

Mr. and Mrs. K have a $5 million estate and understand that the tax exposure exceeds $1.5 million. They have two reasons for doing nothing. First, they profess disinterest–"it's the kids' problem." Second, they believe that Congress and the President will cooperate and extend the $5 million level of estate tax protection. At worst, they believe that the protection will settle in at $3.5 million, as it was in 2009.

Maybe they are right. Maybe members of Congress and the President will compromise and accommodate one another. Maybe the President will act to reduce estate tax exposure and revenues.

Objectively, it is wise to be conservative and plan for the worst while hoping for the best. This means that planning steps should be taken. If you view it as "the kids' problem," involve them in the process and let them know about the tax exposure. If they are financially able, they may be willing to pay for tax advice on your behalf.

"But why should the frugal and thrifty among the rich be taxed heavily on their death beds, while the spendthrifts who live luxuriously are not?"
—Edward J. McCaffery

<u>Think about the grandkids</u>.

"Your kids are OK–they have their issues.
But the grandkids are perfect!"
—M.G.

Unless your children are very secure financially, inheritance matters. You may feel that they will get along just fine, regardless of what you leave them. But if you think about the possible needs of your grandchildren and great-grandchildren, you may come to a different conclusion.

The cost of living and the cost of housing, in particular, are prohibitively high in many communities. Yet, we want our children and grandchildren to live nearby. We may have to help them with a down payment on a home they otherwise could not afford. This is critically important for our quality of life.

"Study after study shows that we are healthier and
happier if our kids live nearby and are part of our
everyday lives."
—M.G.

If you do not want to deal with estate tax for the benefit of your children, do so for the benefit of your grandchildren. You may help pay for the best quality education, regardless of expense. This also means that you will also include Dynasty Trusts in your estate plan for the benefit of your children–to avoid estate tax exposure when they pass, in the distant future. See Chapter 7.

"Don't have children. Have grandchildren."
—Gore Vidal

2. You are reluctant or unwilling to pay legal fees

"That's how smart people avoid tax and keep their money. They throw a few bucks at attorneys and CPAs and get good advice."
—Len Tillem, lawyer and radio talk show host

"[Estate taxes are not really taxes but] penalties imposed on those who neglect to plan ahead or who retain unskilled estate planners."
—Henry Aaron and Alicia Munnell

It does cost money to plan properly. It can be challenging to write that check to pay the lawyer, particularly since you live frugally "and have kept every Cool Whip container that crossed your threshold!"

The problem is that you must actually write a check to pay for legal advice, while the dramatically higher costs of other professional services are effectively invisible even though you are, in fact, paying them.

Let's get some perspective on this question of attorney fees. Consider the very real case of Mr. and Mrs. H.

> Example 5-4: Getting perspective on professional fees
>
> Mr. and Mrs. H have a $6 million estate. They have $2 million under professional management. Also, they just sold their $2 million house and are now living in a continuing care retirement community (CCRC).

They are worried about estate tax exposure. They understand that their exposure exceeds $2 million. They saw a skilled, competent tax attorney, who said the fees for a plan to address tax planning would likely exceed $10,000.[4]

Mr. H was outraged. He shopped around and found an attorney who said it would cost only $4,000 to do his AB trust and estate planning. He hired this attorney, paid $4,000, and was very gratified.

So Mr. and Mrs. H saved $6,000 on legal fees and achieved no tax planning. Remember: an AB revocable trust protects no more than $2 million as of 2013. They accepted over $2 million in estate tax exposure. *A $10, 000 investment in sophisticated planning would have saved as much as $2 million in estate tax.*

Did Mr. H think about other fees that he is paying?

His **money manager** charges a fee of 1% of managed assets each year. He is paying his money manager $20,000 per year. On top of that, the mutual funds in which his assets were placed generated additional management fees. The money manager has not been great, underperforming the S&P 500 by 2%. "An Index fund would have better," Mr. H says. Over the last 5 years, his money manager's fees exceeded

---

4   Tax advice of this nature is typically tax deductible, so the net fee is dramatically less.

$100,000. But Mr. H never had to write a check since the fees were periodically deducted from his account. The same is true for mutual fund fees that never see the light of day. He did not think about these fees and did not complain.

Realtor fees for the sale of his house were 6% of the $2 million purchase price. The house sold within one week of going on the market. "It sold itself," says Mr. H, because of its location and condition. Realtor fees were $120,000. It never occurred to Mr. H to negotiate these fees. He did not have to write a check, as the realtors collected fees out of escrow. He did not complain about this $120,000 fee.

With some proceeds of the house sale, Mr. and Mr. H decided to invest in an annuity. They contacted their **insurance agent**, who sold them the annuity. The commission collected by the insurance agent was $30,000. Mr. H did not have to write a check, so he did not complain. The fee was invisible.

So, some $270,000 in money management and realtor fees and annuity commissions were paid by Mr. and Mrs. H without a thought. Yet, he refused to pay $10k for tax planning and advice that would save his family as much as $2 million.

"We pay more attention to the cost of toilet paper than we do to the cost and benefits of tax advice."
—M.G.

Use online trust services at your peril.

Sophisticated consumers know better, but it can be tempting to avoid the cost of a skilled and experienced estate planning attorney. Online services do not pretend to offer tax planning advice. They stick with the "basics," which may be adequate for individuals with small estates. Even then, scores of difficult questions are not asked, as this would make simple "fill out the form" planning impossible.

For example, individuals utilizing this approach are asked to identify successor trustees. The challenging and demanding responsibilities of serving as a successor trustee are not explained. The "pros and cons" of naming two children, for example, as a co-trustees are not explained. Experienced estate planning attorneys often devote 15 to 30 minute discussions to this topic alone because it is so important.

Countless other issues require discussion and thoughtful resolution. More time may be devoted to choosing your next automobile than to terms of your revocable trust, which is profoundly important for the benefit of your spouse, your children, and your grandchildren.

You have worked a lifetime to grow your estate. You want to protect it for your family for generations. You can only do this if you get good advice from a truly qualified attorney. See Chapter 8 to get even more perspective.

3. You are unwilling to give up control of your assets

You may be comfortable with the idea of giving up ownership or control of significant assets if there is a significant tax advantage in doing so.

Alternatively, it may make you uncomfortable. This is perhaps more likely if you have business or rental properties that you own and actively manage. More simply, you may not like the idea of giving up ownership because it would make you feel less independent, less in control. Perhaps you would feel too dependent on your children if you give a substantial portion of your estate to them.

> *"'A gift is a gift. There can be no strings attached.'*
> *Not necessarily so!"*
> *—Francis A. La Poll, Esq.*

If you make simple, direct gifts to your children, you have given up ownership and control. But there are other ways of removing assets from your estate without giving up control. For example, you can place rental properties in a family limited partnership, give your children up to 99% of the partnership, but *keep control and a substantial management fee by being the general partner*. You can achieve this same result with other planning tools, as well.

4. You want to keep your money for travel, enjoyment, and the cost of long-term care

You want to do tax planning, and you trust your kids, but you have a lot of life left to live. You want to have ample resources under your control so that you can pay for any enjoyable activity, including international travel, that strikes your fancy. You want to do as you please!

You may also be concerned about the cost of long-term care, which can include help at home, assisted living, residential care, and skilled nursing care.

It is indeed fundamental that you should have freedom from financial worries as you live your life. Tax planning is not an "all or nothing" proposition. Rather, it is a matter of identifying your goals and crafting a plan that accommodates as many of them as possible.

Here are some approaches you could take:

- Retain significant assets, notwithstanding tax implications.
- Convey assets to your children, who then place some or most of them in a trust or trusts established for your benefit. There will therefore be ample resources available for anything you need, with a focus on maintaining your current standard of living.
- Develop a comprehensive plan, using the planning tools in Chapters 6, 7, and 8, to achieve the plan that most pleases you.
- Many other approaches can be taken.

"The primary goal of estate planning is not the avoidance of tax. The primary goal is to assure you of a wonderful quality of life. Tax avoidance and asset protection objectives must be harmonized with this overriding objective."
—M.G.

B. Planning for Long-Term Care

Anything can happen. Even we Boomers have to acknowledge this truth. High-quality long-term care services may prove to be essential. You may need help at home from a professional caregiver. You may need to live in an assisted living facility, where help is available if you need it. At some point, you may need to be in a skilled nursing facility. All of these are expensive, costing as much as $10,000 per month or more. In New York City, for example, some skilled nursing facilities cost over $15,000 per month.

Consider purchasing long-term care insurance. Comprehensive policies allow you to use the benefits for home care, assisted living, or skilled nursing care.

If you do not have such insurance when you need it, you will either have to pay out of your own pocket (self-insure) or qualify for Medicaid; known as Medi-Cal in California. [5] It can pay all or most of the cost of nursing home care. Medicaid typically does not pay for assisted living. In most states, it does not pay for home care services, except on a very limited basis.

---

[5]   This topic, "Planning for Long-Term Care and Asset Protection," is itself as complicated and rewarding as protective tax planning. Information about Medicaid/Medi-Cal planning to protect assets when facing the cost of long-term care is available at www.gilfix.com. Alternatively, call the office of Gilfix & La Poll Associates at (800) 244-9424.

Chapter 6: Estate Tax Planning—The Fundamentals

For assets to be exposed to the estate tax, they must be in your "estate" at the time of your death. If they are removed from your estate prior to your death, they avoid this tax.

If it were this simple, you would simply give away all of your assets before your passing and eliminate this tax. It is not this simple, as there are limitations on gifting. Yet, it can be done.

If you give away too much money to take advantage of appropriate tools, or do it too simplistically, you may have to pay a "gift tax."[6] This tax is the same as the estate tax rate, currently 35%.

---

[6] A **federal gift tax return** (Form 709) must be filed with the IRS if you gift more than $13,000 to any individual in a calendar year. This tax return reports such gifts and indicates why no gift tax has to be paid.

Planning Notes: If you make gifts—make no mistakes!

Cost Basis

If you transfer assets other than cash, note that the recipient takes your "cost basis" in the gifted assets. While rarely a reason to forego gifting when estate taxes are to be avoided, it is a factor to consider.

Special Needs Trust

If you have a child or grandchild with special needs, gifts should not be made directly to that child. Instead, a Special Needs Trust should be created for the benefit of the child, and assets are transferred to that trust.

Dynasty Trust

Most gifts or transfers should be made to Dynasty Trusts. See Chapter 7.

Here are the most obvious, fundamental steps that can be taken to reduce the size of your taxable estate.

A. The annual exclusion

You can give away up to $13,000 per year—to as many people as you like—without having to report it to the IRS. Such gifts have no impact on your lifetime gift and estate tax protection. A married couple can therefore give $26,000 to each of their children and each of their grandchildren year after year with out reporting such gifts. In fact, these gifts can be made to anyone, regardless of his or her relationship to you.

Receipt of these gifts, like the receipt of all gifts, is not a taxable event. The recipient simply keeps and enjoys the money.

The simplest way to use this opportunity is to give cash. You can be more creative and give away stock, partnership interests, and fractional interests in real property.

Be careful about using *Uniform Transfer to Minor's Act (UTMA)* accounts for these gifts, though bank tellers so often recommend them. If you do, you will likely be advised to serve as "custodian" of such accounts. This sounds good because you will have the power to decide if and how to invest the money. There are, however, two potential problems. First, the full value of these accounts are counted as part of your taxable estate if you die while still serving as custodian. If you have a taxable estate, $100,000 in such accounts will generate estate tax in the area of $55,000 in 2013. This is tax on money you do not even own!

Second, your kids or grandkids receive the money when they are either 18 or 21. Is that wise? Will the money go to scuba gear, a hot car (the "Lamborghini Effect"), or be used for drugs or alcohol? Will the recipient drop out of college "just for a while" to backpack in Europe?

It is typically better to give to trusts or other entities that will allow you or some other trusted person to control the funds. The trust can end when the child attains a more mature age and the trust assets are then distributed to him. Alternatively, the trust can allow the trustee to decide how to use the money and when the young beneficiary is to be given control or ownership.

"Annual exclusion" gifts can not be made to either Special Needs Trusts or Dynasty Trusts. They can be made to properly drafted "Crummey Trusts," a topic beyond the scope of this book.

B. The remarkable $5 million giving opportunity (What this book is all about!)

In 2012, you can give away up to $5 million without paying any gift tax. As with annual exclusion gifts, receipt of such gifts is not a taxable event. There is no income tax to pay. This means that a married couple can give away $10 million in 2012. With sophisticated planning, described below, substantially more can in fact be given and, thereby, removed from your taxable estate.

Such gifts must be reported on a gift tax return (I.R.S. Form 709). If you use this giving opportunity, you are exhausting your estate tax protection on a dollar for dollar basis.

Example 6-1: $3 million estate, $1 million gift

Mr. May had an estate valued at $3 million. He gives his daughter $1 million in 2012. He reports the gift to the IRS. His death occurs in 2014 when the level of estate tax protection is only $1 million. Since he made a $1 million gift previously, he has zero estate tax protection remaining. The full $2 million still in his estate is exposed to estate tax. The tax exceeds $1 million. His gift was not necessarily a mistake, but he achieved very little.

Example 6-2: $3 million estate, $3 million gift

Ms. Johnson has a $3 million estate and gives away her entire estate in 2012 to her two children. She reports the gifts to the IRS. Upon her death in 2014, when the level of estate tax protection is only $1 million, she has no assets remaining in her estate. No estate tax must be paid; her entire estate avoided tax exposure.

Example 6-3: $6 million estate, $5 million gift

Mr. Long has a $6 million estate and gives $5 million to his children in 2012. He reports the gift to the IRS. His death occurs in 2014, when the level of protection is only $1 million. His remaining estate is subject to estate tax, but the $5 million previously transferred escapes estate tax exposure. Had he retained all assets, well over $2.5 million would be lost to the estate tax.

The tax avoidance benefits of this opportunity are enormous. They should be considered by every unmarried person with an estate in excess of $1 million. They should be considered by every couple with an estate in excess of $2 million.

Such giving must also be carefully considered. It should not be done if you will lose sleep at night or otherwise compromise your quality of life.

C. Pay tuition for relatives, anyone

You may pay the cost of tuition for anyone, related or not. This includes preschool and elementary school, as well as college and postgraduate education. You must pay the institution directly, rather than give your grandchild the money and have him or her pay the tuition. This is separate from and in addition to all other planning options.

This opportunity does not include the cost of room and board. It is separate from and in addition to other opportunities defined in this chapter.

D. Pay medical bills for relatives, anyone

You may pay medical bills for anyone. You must directly pay the provider—the physician, the hospital, and/or the clinic. There is no limit and doing so does not erode or reduce your lifetime gift and estate tax protections.

Remember: do not give the money to the individual who incurred the bill so she can pay it. Leave her out of it and pay the bill directly.

Chapter 7: Dynasty or Family Protection Trusts

Dynasty Trusts "offer big tax savings and can help protect family money from creditors and ex-spouses."
—Wall Street Journal, August 20, 2003

This is a trust that you must establish for the benefit of your child or children. The only exception, parenthetically, is if you have a child with special needs, in which case a Special Needs Trust is required.

When you leave assets to your children, you have two alternative approaches that you can take. You can leave the assets directly to them or you can leave assets to a trust or trusts you establish for their benefit. If you leave the assets directly to them, they have complete control of them and they are exposed to litigation and other potential assaults. More importantly, the assets become part of your children's estates. Upon their passing, all of these assets are again exposed to estate tax.

"Whenever possible, we take a multi-generational approach."
—M.G.

The alternative is to establish a Dynasty Trust, also known as a Family Protection Trust, for the benefit of each child. We recommend this approach because of the benefits and protections derived from such trusts. These protections are in three powerful areas.

A. Divorce Protection: "Pre-Nup" or "Post-Nup" Planning for Your Kids

Any divorce attorney will tell you that, after a married person inherits assets, all or most of those assets will be held in both names after a few years go by. This happens because life goes on, not because the son-in-law or daughter-in-law is a conniving person. Your child and her husband may move their assets to a new entity, such as Schwab, or put them under management with a new money manager. When this is done, they will be asked how the accounts are to be titled. A couple's assets are somewhat logically presumed to be shared assets in such circumstances. It may automatically be placed in both names.

They may also decide to buy a new house or a second property. A title company may automatically put such property in both names, sometimes asking and sometimes not. The point is that inherited assets, more typically than not, end up in both your child's name and his or her spouse's name. If there is ever a divorce, those assets are divided equally. Half of your child's inherited assets can be lost in divorce proceedings.

"You would roll over in your grave!"
—M.G.

If you instead leave assets to Dynasty Trusts established for the benefit of your son or daughter, the assets are segregated and will remain with your child even if he or she someday endures a divorce. The assets are therefore preserved for your child and your grandchildren. They remain in your "bloodline."

In a very real sense, creating such trusts is tantamount to preparing an antenuptial (also knowns as a prenuptial) or postnuptial agreement for your child. You will spare your child the need to have a difficult discussion with his or her spouse about why assets cannot be placed into both of their names. When asked, your daughter replies: "I would love to, but I can't. Everything is in an irrevocable trust and I can't change its terms." Let her (gratefully) blame you!

B. Litigation Protection

If you leave assets directly to your child, they will be in his name and exposed to collection if someone successfully sues him. If you instead leave assets in a Dynasty Trust, they enjoy a very high level of asset protection. This is because the assets do not belong to your child. A person successfully suing your daughter will then have to commence a separate action in an effort to break the trust and reach trust assets. At minimum, this structure provides enormous settlement value, as do offshore trusts.

Litigation protection is maximized if someone other than your child serves as trustee of the Dynasty Trust. In most situations, however, litigation is not a major fear and it is appropriate to let your child serve as trustee, perhaps stepping aside as trustee during the pendency of any legal proceedings if there is a challenge.

The extent of litigation protection depends on the law in your state and how the trust is written.

C. Estate Tax Protection for Your Children and Grandchildren

This is the best known benefit of a Dynasty Trust. It also explains why such trusts are sometimes referred to as "GST" trusts or "generation-skipping" trusts.

> Example 7-1: Saving millions for the grandkids—GST tax planning
>
> You transfer $5 million to a properly drafted Dynasty Trust for the benefit of your son in the year 2012. Only somewhat optimistically, assume that the $5 million asset grows to be worth $12 million at the time of your son's passing in the distant future. *The full $12 million will pass intact for the benefit of your son's children, your grandchildren. None of it will be exposed to estate tax*. This quite literally achieves the avoidance of over $6 million in estate tax.

Tax law includes a "generation-skipping transfer" tax. If you transfer too much to your grandchildren, this 35% GST tax is imposed on top of and in addition to the gift tax. Generally speaking, the amount that can be passed along to or for the benefit of grandchildren without exposure to this tax is the same as the level of estate tax protection. Since $5 million is protected from GST tax exposure in 2012, that amount can be conveyed to a Dynasty Trust. These assets, including their growth, will not be included in the estates of your child or your grandchildren, since the Dynasty Trust structure remains in place for them, as well.

Example 7-2: Allocating GST Tax (2012); $3 Million Estate

You transfer $3 million to a Dynasty Trust for the benefit of your daughter. The full $3 million will enjoy GST protection. The entire amount, perhaps $7 million or $8 million at the time of your daughter's death, will pass without exposure to estate tax. See the following illustration.

ILLUSTRATION IV
2012 Dynasty Trust GST Allocation
Gift to Trust: $3 Million

GST Tax Protected $3 million	Unprotected by GST Protection: $0
— Unlimited Growth (e.g. $7-8 million)	— Zero because under $5 million transferred
— Excluded from daughter's taxable estate	
— Passes to her children free of tax	

Get it? This can be millions and millions of dollars protected from estate tax exposure for your future great grandchildren and beyond. What a legacy!

If the level of estate tax protection is only $1 million, as it will be in 2013 and beyond, only $1 million can be passed along to a Dynasty Trust to capture this benefit. If more than $1 million is transferred by gift or by death to a Dynasty Trust in and after 2013, only the first million dollars will capture this protection. Its growth will similarly be protected. All other assets in the Dynasty Trust will be included in your child's estate at the time of his or her passing.

Example 7-3: Allocating GST Tax (2013); $3 Million Estate

Your death occurs in 2013. You are single and you leave a total of $3 million to a Dynasty Trust for the benefit of your daughter. $1 million will enjoy GST tax protection. It will be separately allocated and designated. Those assets will likely be invested for growth. If that million grows to be worth, say, $4 million at the time of your daughter's death, the entire $4 million will pass without exposure to estate tax. The other $2 million dollars, which does not enjoy GST protection, will more likely be utilized and enjoyed by your daughter because whatever is left will be included in her estate at the time of her passing.

ILLUSTRATION V
2013 Dynasty Trust GST Allocation

$3 Million Estate

GST Protected $1 million	Unprotected by GST Protection: $2 million
— Unlimited Growth — Excluded from child's taxable estate	— Full amount included in child's taxable estate and exposed to estate tax

* * *

Who will be the trustee of this trust? If your child is a capable money manager, he or she can be the trustee of her own trust. If there is some question about ability to manage assets, you can name another individual or entity to serve as trustee or co-trustee.

Rule Against Perpetuities: In most states, these trusts and the estate tax protection lasts for perhaps three generations. It is limited by the "Rule Against Perpetuities." Some states have eliminated or substantially extended the Rule, allowing Dynasty Trusts and their tax and other protections to last for multiple generations.

Regardless of whether you fund Dynasty Trusts by gift or bequest, they are an essential component of a good estate plan. Throughout this publication, we assume that they will be integrated into your planning.

Chapter 8: Advanced Estate Planning—What You Can Do to Protect Your Estate

"Anyone may so arrange his affairs that his taxes shall be as low as possible; he is not bound to choose that pattern which will best pay the Treasury; there is not even a patriotic duty to increase one's taxes."
—Learned Hand, renowned federal judge

In this chapter, I introduce you to the more powerful and available planning approaches that can reduce or eliminate your estate tax exposure. They complement the "basic" planning steps outlined in Chapter 6.

A. The Irrevocable Life Insurance Trust (ILIT)—Supercharging Inherited Wealth

You may have been advised to purchase a $2 million life insurance policy so that your children will have liquid assets to pay the estate tax that will be due upon your death. If you do this, you are compounding the problem, not addressing it.

As explained above, life insurance death benefits are part of your taxable estate if you had any "incidents of ownership" in the policy. If you do, the $2 million is added to other assets that you own as the total value of your estate is calculated. The $2 million life insurance policy will itself generate over $1 million in estate tax exposure if you have a taxable estate.

You have such "incidents of ownership" if you own the policy, pay the premiums, or reserve the right to change the beneficiaries. Even if you do not, the entire amount can become part of your estate if you name your "estate" as the beneficiary of your policy.

If you create an irrevocable life insurance trust (ILIT) and properly manage it, the death benefit will not be included as part of your estate, regardless of how large it is. If you have a $2 million life insurance policy, the full $2 million is distributed to the beneficiaries. If you have a $10 million life insurance policy, the full $10 million is distributed to the beneficiaries intact.

This irrevocable trust is typically established by you. You name an independent third party to be the trustee of the trust.

The trustee obtains a life insurance policy on your life. Each year, you write checks to the trustee in amounts that typically do not exceed $13,000 for every individual who is named as a beneficiary of the trust.

You explain to the trustee in writing that these gifts are available to the individuals, presumably your children or grandchildren. The trustee informs your children or grandchildren of these gifts and gives them the opportunity to withdraw the money. If they do not, the trustee can use those funds to pay the annual premiums.

By actually making these funds available to the beneficiaries, they qualify for the $13,000 "annual exclusion." The transferred funds are therefore removed from your estate and efficiently utilized to pay life insurance premiums. Because you have no "incidents of ownership" over the policy that is owned by the insurance trust, the death benefit is not part of your taxable estate.

Example 8-1: $5 million ILIT

Mr. Wong creates an ILIT, naming his daughter as the trustee. The trustee obtains a $5 million life insurance policy on Mr. Wong, who must pass a physical examination and otherwise qualify for life insurance. The annual premiums are $65,000. Mr. Wong has five children. He writes five checks in the amount of $13,000 made payable to his trust. He instructs the trustee in writing that these gifts are for his children. The trustee writes a letter to each child, informing the child of the gift and of the opportunity to request and obtain the money from the trustee. The children are given 30 days to claim their money. They do not. The trustee then uses the $65,000 to pay the annual premium. This is done year after year, with careful and appropriate documentation.

Result: Even though Mr. Wong has a large, taxable estate at the time of his death, the $5 million death benefit is distributed to his children, $1 million each, completely free from estate tax exposure.

Example 8-2: $30 million ILIT

This example supercharges insurance and ILIT planning.

Assume that Mr. Black's estate is valued at $30 million. He knows that the estate tax will exceed $14 million if his death occurs in 2013, when only $1 million can be protected. He decides to transfer $5 million worth of assets to an Irrevocable Life Insurance Trust, exhausting his lifetime gifting opportunity. Using income from ILIT assets, the trustee of the trust obtains and pays annual premiums on a $10 million life insurance policy. Remaining in his estate is $25 million.

If Mr. Black does nothing further, $25 million is exposed to estate tax if death occurs in 2013 or thereafter. The tax is approximately $13,750,000. Not included in his estate, and therefore protected for the next generation, are both the $10 million life insurance benefit and the $5 million originally transferred into the ILIT. By this approach, he almost doubles the assets left for the benefit of his children.

ILLUSTRATION VI
Single client Mr. Black

Estimated Net Worth: $30,000,000

	2012: Tax Planning with ILIT	2013: No Tax Planning
Estimated Net Worth	**$30,000,000**	**$30,000,000**
Exemption	-$5,000,000	-$1,000,000
Taxable Estate	$25,000,000	$29,000,000
55% Estate Tax (2013)	$13,750,000	$15,950,000
Subtotal	$11,250,000	$13,050,000
Add back	$5,000,000	$1,000,000
Add in tax-free life insurance	$10,000,000	
TOTAL LEFT IN ESTATE	**$26,250,000**	**$14,050,000**

NET: $12,200,000 more is preserved with ILIT Planning

* * *

Example 8-3: Saving $7 million and more using ILIT

Ms. White also has a taxable estate. It is valued at $10 million. If she does no planning, $1 million will be protected after 2012. Over $4 million is lost to estate tax.

Assume that she decides to transfer $5 million to an ILIT, permanently removing it from her taxable estate. Five million dollars therefore remain in her taxable estate. Income from trust assets is used to pay premiums on a $5 million life insurance policy. At the time of her passing, over $2.5 million are lost to estate taxes.

Protected for her children are the $5 million death benefit and the remaining $5 million in assets still in the irrevocable trust. Assets left for the benefit of her children are more than double what they would have been if she simply retained all assets in her name.

ILLUSTRATION VII
Single client Ms. White

Estimated Net Worth: $10,000,000

How much will be left in the Estate?

	2012: Tax Planning with ILIT	2013: No Tax Planning
Estimated Net Worth	**$10,000,000**	**$10,000,000**
Exemption	-5,000,000	—1,000,000
Taxable Estate	$5,000,000	$9,000,000
55% Estate Tax (2013)	$2,750,000	$4,950,000
Subtotal	$2,250,000	$4,050,000
Add back	$5,000,000	$1,000,000
Add in tax-free life insurance	$5,000,000	
TOTAL LEFT IN ESTATE	**$12,250,000**	**$5,050,000**

NET: $7,200,000 more preserved with ILIT Planning

**Use of Dynasty or Family Protection Trust: As described in Chapter 7, all of these ILIT creators also create one Dynasty Trust for the benefit of each of their children. Rather than have the death benefits flow directly to their children, they will instead go to the Dynasty Trusts, which will be explicitly named as beneficiaries of the insurance trust. In this way, inherited assets can avoid exposure to estate tax when the children pass. This can save them—and the grandchildren—millions of dollars in estate tax. *Indeed, virtually all assets passed from one generation to the next should go into Dynasty Trusts.*

B. Family Limited Partnership: giving away much more than $5 million

A Family Limited Partnership (FLP) is an entity that you can create for a family business, rental property, or other actively managed assets. It offers many management and asset protection benefits. It also creates opportunities for the transfer of family wealth to the next generation.

There are two types of partners in an FLP. There is the "general partner," who has control of the partnership. There are also the "limited partners," who have no control.

A properly structured FLP allows you to "discount" the value of assets that are transferred from you, the owner of the assets, to your children and grandchildren. This well-established approach therefore allows you to leverage both the $13,000 annual exclusion and the $5 million lifetime gifting opportunity to substantially higher levels.

It is only successful, appropriately, if there is a legitimate business purpose or benefit.

How does discounting work? If you own a portion of an asset but have no control over it, its value is obviously limited. You may need cash and want to sell the asset, but you cannot do so. It is not your choice, and it is not within your power. Alternatively, you may have control of an asset and give a partial interest to one of your children. Because you have complete control, the value of the interests owned by your children is limited and compromised. They are completely passive and can neither access nor benefit from their limited interest unless you cooperate. Generally, this is why tax law may allow you to discount the value of an asset in an entity like an FLP.

Example 8-4: Give up control, keep income.

Assume that you place rental property valued at $1 million in an FLP. You transfer a 1% interest to your daughter. You keep a 99% interest, which means that you will retain virtually all of the net income. You name your daughter as the general partner. She therefore has complete management and control of the FLP asset. At the time of your passing, a discount of perhaps 35% to 45% can typically be taken. While the market value of 99% of the FLP assets may approach $1 million, a 40% discount means that the value *for estate tax purposes* is only $600,000. In this hypothetical example, over $200,000 in estate tax is avoided.

A discount is allowed because you have given up complete control of the partnership and, therefore, the underlying assets. You did not have the power, for example, to decide about capital improvements or when to sell the property. Only your daughter, the general partner, has this power. The value of this asset in your estate is therefore substantially compromised and reduced.

Example 8-5: Give up ownership but keep control.

You devoted your life to a business that is now successful and valued at $5 million. Your son works in the business and is the likely successor. Because you have a large estate, this $5 million asset will generate an estate tax in excess of $2.5 million. You create an FLP and transfer ownership of the business into the FLP.

You want to remove this valuable asset from your estate, but you also want to retain control—for at least five more years. You will name yourself as the general partner and your son as the limited partner. You immediately begin transferring limited partnership interests to your son.

Because your son is a limited partner, he has no control of the partnership assets. Moreover, his limited partnership interest is virtually unmarketable. Who would buy a portion of the family partnership when you are still in complete control? To attract any independent buyer, the value of any interest would have to be very substantially reduced. For these and other reasons, the value of any transferred interest is substantially discounted.

Example 8-6: Use the $13,000 annual exclusion to leverage the transfer of partnership assets.

Rather than transfer partnership units valued at $13,000 to your son, you instead transferred $21,500 worth of partnership assets and discount the value by 40%. The value of this transfer is therefore $12,900. Because it is less than the annual exclusion, it is not reportable to the IRS. Also, it does not affect or diminish your lifetime estate tax protection.

Example 8-7: Use the current $5 million giving opportunity to transfer partnership units.

You can transfer 99% of the partnership units, valued at $4,950,000, to your son as the limited partner. If you take a 40% discount, $1,980,000 worth of the partnership effectively disappears for transfer tax purposes. After the discount, the value of this gift is only $2,970,000. This gift is reported on a federal gift tax return, Form 709. You did exhaust more than half of your $5 million gift and estate tax protection. The benefit: you avoided over $1 million in estate tax, at minimum. This further allows for greater gifts of other assets during 2012. You also transferred effective ownership of the partnership at its current appraised value. If the business grows in value in the future, 99% of the growth is in your son's estate, rather than yours. It therefore avoids estate tax exposure at the time of your death.

How was the size of the discount determined? An independent professional, such as a CPA, reviews the partnership agreement. The size of the discount is based on the specific elements or provisions of the partnership agreement. Criteria relied upon by the IRS to determine the size of the discount are no secret. The independent professional produces a written, detailed appraisal of the partnership and proffers the size of the discount that can legitimately be taken.

In the context of FLPs—or virtually all transfers—shares or interests are best transferred into *Dynasty or Family Protection Trusts for the benefit of a child, children, or grandchildren*. In this way, asset protection benefits are captured and all or most of the value of transferred interests are protected from estate tax exposure on the passing of your children. See Chapter 7 for a complete discussion of Dynasty Trusts.

C. Limited Liability Corporation

A Limited Liability Corporation (LLC) is conceptually similar to the Family Limited Partnership in that it, too, allows for the discounting of interests when properly structured.

The LLC is often utilized for asset protection purposes. It is designed, quite literally, to limit your liability in the event that litigation focuses on an asset within the LLC. Limited Liability Corporation shares or interests can be transferred with similar discounting opportunities.

D. Fractional Shares of Real Property

If you own an entire interest in real property, it is obvious that the entire value is in your estate at the time of your passing. What if you only own a 90% interest? If the market value of the property is $1 million, is your interest valued at $900,000 for estate tax purposes?

No. If you do not own an entire interest, your control and your ability to take such steps as refinancing or selling the property is compromised. As a result, you can typically take a 15% to 30%[7] discount when determining the value of your interest for estate tax purposes.

Example 8-8: Fractional share and discounting

You transfer a 10% interest in your $10 million rental property to your daughter's Family Protection Trust for her benefit. The 90% interest you retained would be valued at $9 million if only market value is considered. The limitations that flow from owning only a fractional share—anything less than 100%—allow your estate to discount your interest by perhaps 25% at the time of your passing. After the discount is taken, the value of this interest is reduced to only $6,750,000, removing $2,250,000 from your taxable estate. Over $1,200,000 in estate taxes are thereby avoided.

---

[7] The reader is again reminded that examples are simplified for understanding. Although estimates of discounting are generally accurate, no effort is made to provide either a detailed analysis or precise numbers. My goal is to convey the concept, not the details.

<u>Caveat</u>: Implementation of this approach is more complicated than the simple transfer of a fractional share interest to one or more others—or to their Family Protection Trusts. Documentation and agreements must address such issues as the "partition action," which allows a partial owner to effectively force the sale of the property.

E. Personal Residence Trust (PRT, QPRT)

Your home may be your most valuable asset. It may be valued from $900,000 to $5,000,000. You may also have a vacation home with comparable value. If these assets are in your estate at the time of your passing, they alone can generate an enormous estate tax liability. This is inevitable in and after 2013 when the level of estate tax protection drops to only $1 million per person.

The Personal Residence Trust (PRT) is an irrevocable trust into which you transfer your home as a means of transferring ownership to your children or, as always, to Family Protection or Dynasty Trusts established for their benefit. Again, this approach is utilized because it enables you to significantly "discount" the value of the transferred residence.

Variations are also known as Grantor Retained Interest Trusts (GRITs) and Qualified Personal Residence Trusts (QPRTs).

<u>Example 8-9: Protecting the Residence</u>

You have a residence valued at $2 million. You have other assets and you have a taxable estate. If you own the residence at the time of your passing, by which time it has increased in value to $4 million, it will generate an estate tax in excess of $2 million.

You instead transfer the property into this irrevocable trust, the PRT. The trust provides that you will retain effective control and use of the property for a designated number of years, perhaps 10. At the end of the 10 year period, the trust terminates and the property is distributed to the Dynasty Trusts established for the benefit of your children. At that point, while you are still living, your children's trusts become the owners of the property. The property is removed from your estate.

What is the value of the gift of this $4 million residence? Because your children have to wait 10 years before they obtain ownership, the gift is not worth even $2 million at the time you transfer it into the trust. At that point in time, they have an expectancy or a future interest and nothing more. Because of this delay, the value of the gift at the time it is made is discounted by approximately 50%.

The size of the discount depends primarily on the length of the term. The longer the term, the bigger the discount because the recipients have to wait a longer period of time before they obtain ownership. The shorter the term, the smaller the discount because they will obtain ownership much sooner.

In the above example, you may wind up giving away a $4 million house, but it is treated as a gift of only $1 million. The technique makes $3 million disappear, saving $1,650,000 in estate taxes.

Consider this analogy: if you give a one dollar bill to your son, he takes it and can immediately spend it. This is a completed gift valued at $1. If you instead placed the one dollar bill in a sealed envelope and set it aside for your son, but provide that he does not get it for 10 years, the current value of the gift is substantially less than one dollar. Would your son not rather get $.50 right now rather than wait 10 years to get a $1 bill? Put differently, the current value of the one dollar gift that the recipient will not get for 10 years is worth much less than $1 to the recipient when the envelope is opened.

Similarly, the PRT or QPRT is the sealed envelope. The irrevocable trust holds title to the property until a term of years expires. Only then do the recipients get the property.

A *Wall Street Journal* article entitled "Gifting Your House and Living in It, Too" says this about the QPRT:

> "Plunging real-estate values have made it an opportune time for older homeowners to give property to their children, while realizing big savings on gift and estate taxes."[8]

This trust can also be used for a second residence. A vacation home can therefore be transferred into such a trust, with the same discount benefits. This same technique may also be applied to gifts of other types of

---

[8]   See Mike Spector, "Gifting Your House and Living in It, Too," Wall Street Journal, October 30, 2007.

assets if the beneficiary(ies) of the trust are not lineal descendants. Such trusts can be used to tremendous advantage to shelter gifts to nieces, nephews, and other family members.

F. Intentionally Defective Irrevocable Trust (IDIT)

An IDIT is an irrevocable trust. It is also a "grantor trust," which means that the person establishing the trust, the grantor, must pay income taxes on the income created by the trust. However, the assets in the trust are not includable in the grantor's estate for estate tax purposes.

Here's how it works: a grantor will typically make a small gift to an IDIT with cash or property. The IDIT then buys a valuable asset from the grantor, using the small gift as a "down payment" and covering the rest of the value through a promissory note. Through this transfer, the grantor has "frozen" the value of the asset and has transferred wealth by converting an asset increasing in value into an asset with a fixed yield, such as an interest-bearing note. The IDIT shifts all increase in value above the comparatively low fixed yield out of the grantor (parent's) estate to the trust beneficiaries (children) without gift or estate tax.

The grantor can also discount the value of the asset transferred into the IDIT, for reasons discussed in prior sections. This reduces the fair market value of the asset, as well as the value of the promissory note, often dramatically reducing the amount subject to estate and gift tax.

G. Charitable Trust

A Charitable Trust is an irrevocable trust designed to reduce taxes while benefiting a charity. These trusts are attractive if you also have charitable giving inclinations, although many individuals create and utilize this trust approach exclusively for tax planning and income purposes.

There are two main types of Charitable Trusts: the Charitable Remainder Trust (CRT) and the Charitable Lead Trust (CLT). Both are discussed below.

1. Charitable Remainder Trust (CRT)

Assets are placed in a CRT for a specified time period. During that time period, the beneficiaries, such as your children, receive a certain amount of income. At the end of the time period, the remainder of the trust is donated to the designated charity. The income to your children can be calculated by a percentage of the trust principal, as in the case of the Charitable Remainder Unitrust (CRUT). Alternately, your children can receive a fixed dollar amount each year, as in the Charitable Remainder Annuity Trust (CRAT).

a. <u>Charitable Remainder Unitrust (CRUT)</u>: This approach is particularly appropriate if you have a valuable asset, say a rental property or founders' stock, with low cost basis that is insufficiently productive. You may want to generate more income from the asset by reinvesting the value, but sale of the asset would generate a punishing capital gains tax. This trust allows for the sale of the property without exposure to capital gains tax and the guarantee of lifetime income.

Example 8-10: CRUT increases income, captures income tax benefit

You own a four-plex valued at $1.2 million. The cost basis is only $200,000. If you sell the property, you will have a $1 million capital gain. The federal capital gains tax is 15%. California is one of many states that adds its own capital gains tax, which approaches 10%. Approximately $250,000, or 25% of the capital gain, is therefore lost to capital gains tax exposure. Net proceeds of sale after other costs are reduced to only $950,000. The substantially reduced net proceeds are then invested to give you an income stream. If those assets are invested and you achieve a 4% rate of return, you will have annual income of $34,000, all of which is exposed to income tax.

If you instead establish a CRUT, which is an irrevocable trust, you transfer title of the property into the trust. The trustee then sells the property. Because assets remaining in the trust at the time of your death go to a tax-exempt organization, such as a university, hospital, or your other favorite charity, *capital gains taxes are avoided*. If the net proceeds are therefore $1.1 million, the trust can provide that you are to receive a 4% return for the rest of your life. This will give you $44,000 per year, an increase of $10,000.

If the underlying value of the trust assets increases, your annual income increases because you are guaranteed 4% of the annual value of trust assets. Also beneficial is the fact that income from this trust will enjoy protection from income tax exposure for a number of years because the transfer of this asset into the charitable trust generates a significant income tax deduction that can be used to offset income in the current year and up to five following years.

    b. <u>Charitable Remainder Annuity Trust (CRAT)</u>: You may prefer an annuity approach, which guarantees you a certain number of dollars every year, regardless of growth or decrease in the value of the underlying trust assets. This is to be compared with the Charitable Remainder Unitrust (CRUT), where annual income could decrease if the value of invested assets decreases. The annuity approach is more conservative and more reliable, and is particularly suitable for seniors.

2. **Charitable Lead Trust (CLT)**

    A Charitable Lead Trust can also be used to transfer assets to children or others at a significantly reduced tax liability. The trust makes a fixed "annuity" payment or a variable "unitrust" payment to a charity for a specified term. After the term ends, the assets are either returned to you or are passed on to children or other loved ones. If passed on to heirs, the estate or gift taxes on the value of the gift are reduced or eliminated.

    <u>Example 8-11: Charitable giving and discounting</u>

    You transfer $1,000,000 into a twenty-year charitable lead trust to benefit your favorite charity. The charity receives $50,000 in income annually for the purposes specified by you. At the end of the twenty-year term, your two children receive the trust principal.

For gift tax purposes, only the present value of the "remainder," or the amount your children will ultimately receive, is subject to tax. Treasury tables project the value of the remainder to be about $213,000. Assuming a 6% annual return, and after the annual distributions to the charity, at the end of the twenty-year term the trust principal has grown to about $1,280,500. Your children receive the entire $1,280,500, while your gift tax liability is limited to $213,000. In this case, you have ultimately made a tax-free gift to your children of $1,067,300.

*   *   *

Replace family wealth with an Irrevocable Life Insurance Trust. A properly structured CRT generates a substantially increased income, much of which is protected from income tax exposure. If you would like to replace the wealth that is ultimately transferred to the charity through the CRT rather than passing to your children, you can use a portion of your substantially increased annual income and invest it in a life insurance policy through an Irrevocable Life Insurance Trust (ILIT).

Example 8-12: Charitable giving and wealth replacement

You transfer $20,000 of your increased annual income to an ILIT, as described earlier in this chapter. The ILIT uses those funds to purchase a $1 million life insurance policy. Upon your passing, the full $1 million passes to Dynasty

Trusts established for the benefit of your children.

Be a hero to your favorite charity: If you establish a charitable trust, be sure to inform the charity that is the ultimate beneficiary. They will honor you, invite you to dinners, and generally fete you. Enjoy it!

H. Family Foundation

In conjunction with a CRT or independently, you can create a Family Foundation and transfer unlimited assets into the Foundation to remove them from your taxable estate. You can transfer assets into a Family Foundation while you are living or upon your passing. Either way, the assets avoid estate tax, while lifetime gifts also generate an income tax deduction.

When you create the Foundation, you identify its charitable objectives. Your family members can be officers and directors of the Foundation. To many, this is a means by which family wealth can be enjoyed by future generations in a meaningful way.

I. Grantor Retained Annuity Trust (GRAT)

The Grantor Retained Annuity Trust (GRAT) is an irrevocable trust into which you put assets for a certain term of years. You receive an annuity, or fixed income stream, during that term. When the term is completed, the remaining assets are distributed tax-free to children or other beneficiaries.

The GRAT allows the grantor to leverage transfers to children. As long as the asset in the GRAT increases in value more than the interest rate, the children win.

The value of the gift for gift tax purposes is the value of the property transferred to it, minus the value of the grantor's retained annuity interest. The annuity, or fixed income stream, is a fixed percentage of the initial contribution and, therefore, is a fixed dollar amount. Current historically low interest rates make this approach exceptionally interesting. This type of trust is especially useful if you put in assets that you expect will substantially increase in value in the near future.

> Example 8-13: Retaining income, delayed transfer to children
>
> In July 2009, Mrs. S transfers $1 million into a GRAT. The federal rate for determining the present value of an annuity that month was 2.8% per year. Given the federal tax rules on GRATs, the yearly annuity payment to Mrs. S is set at $116,038 for a term of ten years.
>
> If the assets in the GRAT have a low growth rate equal to the federal tax rate of 2.8% per year, there would not be much benefit to using a GRAT. This is because the required annuity distributions to Mrs. S would eliminate any long-term growth in the GRAT. However, if the assets in the GRAT instead appreciated at 8%, over $450,000 would be passed along to the remainder beneficiaries with no tax exposure.

If the GRAT assets consistently grow faster than the federal tax rate, the GRAT will have a larger remainder to pass to the beneficiaries. This is why GRATs are most beneficial when federal tax rates are low, as now, and the GRAT contains highly appreciating assets.

J. Individual Retirement Accounts (IRAs) and other retirement accounts

You may have significant assets in a retirement account and enjoy deferred income taxation exposure. These assets are part of your taxable estate. They present significant challenges in the context of estate tax avoidance.

If you are charitably inclined, these assets are ideal for ultimate distribution to your favorite tax exempt organization. Individuals with large, taxable estates can *lose up to 80%* of the value of retirement accounts. This is because their value is exposed to estate tax, currently 35% and soon to be as high as 55%. A $1 million IRA in a taxable estate will therefore generate estate tax exposure as high as $550,000. Moreover, IRA funds are exposed to income tax as they are distributed. Those exposed to higher marginal income tax rates can lose over 35% of that income to income tax exposure.

Highly motivated individuals sometimes withdraw significant portions of or all retirement assets and accept the income tax exposure. They then take tax planning steps, outlined above, to protect the value of assets remaining after income tax is paid.

Example 8-14: $500,000 IRA and estate tax

Mr. White has a large, taxable estate. It includes a $500,000 IRA. His annual income is relatively modest, in part because he has invested in tax-free municipal bonds. Over the course of two years, he withdraws 100% of his IRA money. His effective income tax rate is 33%, so $166,667 is paid in income tax as a result of the IRA distributions. He then has $333,333 in his name. He can invest those assets in real property and utilize a Family Limited Partnership, Limited Liability Corporation, or some other entity to substantially reduce his estate tax exposure.

If he has a *Roth IRA*, other opportunities present themselves since distributions are not subject to income tax. He would, nevertheless, hesitate to withdraw all funds because of the beneficial tax treatment that can be passed along to future generations.

K. "Disclaiming" Inherited Assets

"If more people knew about the benefits of a disclaimer, its use would skyrocket."
—M.G.

A radically underused, yet very powerful tax planning tool is a "disclaimer." It is an option that presents itself whenever an individual is inheriting assets. It is a way of saying "No, thank you" to all or any part of an inheritance. If an inheritance is disclaimed, it passes as if the person disclaiming the assets were already deceased. While it may seem illogical or even incredible to reject an inheritance, it can make sense in many situations.

Most typically, a disclaimer should be considered when an individual already has a taxable estate and is about to inherit assets. The inherited assets will add to the taxable estate, exposing over half of those assets to estate tax at the time of death. The disclaimed assets will likely pass to this person's children, so they remain in the family.

> Example 8-15: Rejecting an inheritance and avoiding tax
>
> Mrs. Smith is a widow, 70 years of age, and has an estate valued at $2.5 million. She is concerned that only $1 million of her estate will be protected from estate tax exposure. She is very tax sensitive. She learns that her aunt died and is leaving her an inheritance of $300,000. If she accepts the inheritance, her estate grows by $300,000. Her estate tax exposure also grows by $300,000, adding over $150,000 in potential tax liability.
>
> Mrs. Smith decides to "disclaim" the inheritance. Her aunt's trust provided that, if Mrs. Smith predeceased her aunt, the inheritance would instead go to Mrs. Smith's two children. As a result, the $300,000 passes directly to Mrs. Smith's two children in equal shares. The $300,000 therefore avoids estate tax exposure at Mrs. Smith's passing. Over $150,000 in tax is thereby saved and her children enjoy immediate use of the money.

L. Other Planning Opportunities Exist

We make no effort in this publication to identify every conceivable approach to address estate tax exposure. Nor can we identify which approach is appropriate for any given individual. Many variables that complicate every real life situation must be taken into account when planning to avoid estate tax. The challenge and the opportunity are to implement a plan that is consistent with your values and your goals as an individual and as a family.

Chapter 9: Take Action! Protect Your Estate!

"You are on the right track, but you'll get run over if you don't get up."
—Will Rogers

First, objectively <u>determine the size of your estate</u>. If you did not yet do so, use the "Valuing Your Estate" exercise in Chapter 2. For this exercise, do not use conservative figures. If anything, be optimistic about values. Remember that assets are professionally appraised at the time of your passing. The IRS may audit your estate and challenge values that appear to be artificially low.

Based on the size of your estate, you can easily <u>calculate your estate tax exposure</u>. If you are single, remember that everything over $1 million will be exposed to estate tax. If you are a couple, your revocable trust will only protect $2 million.

Realize that <u>2012 is a year of remarkable opportunity</u>. If you are a married couple, you can give away up to $10 million this year without paying any tax whatsoever. Moreover, the recipients will pay no tax as a result of the transfer. By using discounting techniques, you can leverage this opportunity and give away $18 million or more.

<u>Consult with an experienced tax and estate planning attorney</u>. Only in this way will you be able to identify the planning options that are appropriate for you. You are unique and your plan must be crafted to both reflect and respect your values and your goals. It may include a Family Limited Partnership and the Charitable Remainder Trust. It may include a Personal Residence Trust and fractional share giving. It may include an Irrevocable Life Insurance Trust. It may include all or none of these approaches. The only requirement is that it must effectively and efficiently reduce or eliminate your estate tax exposure in a way that is appropriate for you and your situation.

To contact Michael Gilfix for professional assistance or more information, go to <u>www.gilfix.com</u>.

8 Step Estate Tax Avoidance Checklist

STEP 1: Estimate size of your estate
See Chart B in Chapter 2

STEP 2: Estimate estate tax exposure—as of 2013
Single: 55% of everything over $1 million
Married: 55% of everything over $2 million

STEP 3: Recover from shock. Take deep breaths.
Resolve to act to avoid estate tax

STEP 4: Use Dynasty Trusts for children's inheritance
and/or gifts

STEP 5: Review Chapter 8—summary of planning
options

STEP 6: Obtain professional advice to identify best
options for you

STEP 7: Implement the estate tax avoidance plan of
choice

STEP 8: CELEBRATE!

"Implement a tax avoidance plan that is right for you.
No heads in the sand!"
—M.G.

Bibliography

1. Gilfix, Michael, with Regan, Morgan, and English, *Tax, Estate, and Financial Planning for the Elderly: Forms and Practice*, Matthew Bender, LEXIS-NEXIS (2012, updated bi-annually).

2. Internal Revenue Code of 1986, as amended.

3. Silverman, Rachel Emma, *The Wall Street Journal Complete Estate-Planning Guidebook*, Crown Business, 2011.

4. Yablon, Jeffrey, *As Certain As Death: Quotations about Taxes*, Tax Analysts, April 2010.

Edwards Brothers Malloy
Thorofare, NJ USA
May 3, 2012